WHY SHOULD I CARE ABOUT THE ANCIENT ROMANS?

By Don Nardo

Consultant
Robert. B. Kebric, Ph.D.
Senior Professor of History (Retired)
University of Louisville
Louisville, KY

COMPASS POINT BOOKS
a capstone imprint

Why Should I Care About History? is published by Compass Point Books,
an imprint of Capstone.
1710 Roe Crest Drive, North Mankato, Minnesota 56003
www.capstonepub.com

**Library of Congress Cataloging-in-Publication Data is available on the Library
of Congress website.**
ISBN: 978-0-7565-6420-9 (library binding)
ISBN: 978-0-7565-6564-0 (paperback)
ISBN: 978-0-7565-6421-6 (ebook PDF)

Summary: You might think that what happened in ancient history doesn't
matter to our lives today. Yet we have to thank the ancient Romans for a lot of
discoveries. Their impact is felt in many things from modern engineering and
architecture to socks, fast food restaurants, and movies. Discover how these
inventions got their start in ancient Rome and evolved into things we enjoy
today.

Image Credits:
Alamy: Chronicle, 48, Eugene Sergeev, 56, Imagestate Media PartnersLimited
- Impact Photos, 14, Peter Horree, 44, Universal Images Group North America
LLC, 18, Vito Arcomano, 32; AP Images: Dominique Mollard, 51; Bridgeman
Images: De Agostini Picture Library, 36, Look and Learn/Private Collection,
38; iStockphoto: duncan1890, 35; Mary Evans Picture Library: INTERFOTO/
Nachum T. Gidal, 43; Newscom: akg-images, 49, ImageBROKER/Jochen Tack,
53, World History Archive, 39; Shutterstock: ai-ivanov, 22, Eduardo Estellez, 26,
Fernando Cortes, 29, Jannis Tobias Werner, 24, Marco Rubino, 17, Mazerath, 11,
Peter Hermes Furian, 6, photo-denver, 41, Svetlana Pasechnaya, Cover, (left),
szefei, Cover, (right), ViralMind, 9; Wikimedia: Cnfy1cnfy1, 27

Design Elements:
Shutterstock: Artem Kovalenco

Editorial Credits:
Editor: Gina Kammer; Designer: Tracy McCabe; Media Researcher: Jo Miller;
Production Specialist: Laura Manthe

Printed and bound in the United States of America.
PA99

TABLE OF CONTENTS

CHAPTER 1
ANCIENT IDEAS FOR THE MODERN WORLD........... 5

CHAPTER 2
THE GREATEST PREMODERN BUILDERS.............. 16

CHAPTER 3
ENTERTAINING COMBAT:
THE GLADIATORS.. 28

CHAPTER 4
ANIMAL SHOWS FOR EVERYONE 40

CHAPTER 5
INHERITING THE ROMAN WAY OF WAR.............. 50

GLOSSARY 60
ADDITIONAL RESOURCES 61
SELECT BIBLIOGRAPHY 62
INDEX 64

ANCIENT IDEAS FOR THE MODERN WORLD

As you read this, somewhere in your state firefighters battle a blaze. We all take for granted they will come to our aid if our house catches fire. Similarly, in winter people tend not to worry about freezing in their homes. Instead, they simply turn on the heat. Also, everyone knows how it feels to be hungry and not feel like cooking. When that happens, they rely on neighborhood fast-food restaurants. People take for granted many other customs, ideas, and devices as well. They range from apartment buildings to daily newspapers.

Firefighting, home heating, and fast-food restaurants are so commonplace that few people wonder about their origins. In that regard, they all share two traits. First, none are modern inventions. Second, most of their roots lie in ancient Roman society.

THE ROMAN EMPIRE
in AD 117, at its greatest extent

At its greatest extent, in AD 117, under the emperor Trajan, the Roman Empire included much of Europe and hefty portions of North Africa and the Middle East, some 3.5 million square miles (9 million sq. km) in all.

WHO WERE THE ANCIENT ROMANS, ANYWAY?

The ideas people today inherited from ancient Rome can be seen everywhere. The Romans created one of the most splendid ancient civilizations. They arose in Italy as early as the 700s BC. Over the centuries their empire expanded outward and conquered numerous other peoples. The empire came to include most of Europe along with North Africa and parts of the Middle East. The Romans' mighty realm lasted some twelve centuries in all. Historians generally mark Rome's fall in the late 400s and early 500s as the end of the ancient era and beginning of medieval times.

As a distinct "national group," or people, the Romans were long-lived. From founding to fall, they flourished for about twelve centuries. During those years, they created the biggest empire the world had yet seen. They also built the first large-scale, city-based civilization. In fact, Rome was the first city in history to reach a population of a million.

These impressive feats were not accidental. They happened in part because the Romans were a highly practical people. No matter what challenges they faced, their approach was the same. They sought the simplest, surest way to achieve success. As a result, they found solutions to numerous problems of everyday life. Many of these solutions were so effective that they remain in use today.

GIANT HOUSES OF CARDS

The majority of people today live in cities. But that also means all those people need somewhere to live. That's why we have apartment buildings. The Romans had a similar need. Building the Roman Empire's network of cities took centuries to achieve. It was large-scale and complex. Hence, many challenges the Romans faced over time were connected to city life. One such challenge was how to create enough housing. In the countryside, farmers were spread over vast areas of land. There was plenty of room for each family to live in a separate house, or *domus*. By contrast, space was limited in a city. There was not enough room to build a private domus for every family. So where could the bulk of the population live?

The Romans' answer to that question was to erect large apartment buildings, or blocks, called *insulae*. Some of these buildings had seven or more stories. So a single apartment block could fit far more people than a block of individual single-story houses. The tallest one of these, built in the second century, soared at least ten stories tall. It was the skyscraper of its time.

The average insula was between 250 to 350 feet (76 to 107 meters) wide. Each floor likely had between ten and sixteen small one- or two-room apartments. The total number of apartments was limited because the number of stories was limited. In turn, this limit was related to the building materials involved. These structures were built of stone, wood, and plaster. They lacked the metal skeletons large modern buildings have. Therefore, a tall insulae's lower floors carried an immense amount of weight. Such structures were unstable. They sometimes collapsed. The first-century poet Juvenal joked that an insula was like a giant house of cards.

FACT

The Romans called large apartment buildings, or blocks, insulae. From at least the second century BC on, most residents of the city of Rome dwelled in them. By AD 315 , the city was using 46,602 insulae, compared to only 1,797 private houses, or domus.

Workers digging beneath a church in Rome's central sector during the early 1900s discovered remains of a Roman insula, or apartment block. Parts of four of its original five stories remain intact. The ground floor would often feature shops while apartments were on the upper floors.

MEETING THE NEEDS OF CITY FOLK

Juvenal also mentioned frequent fires in the apartments. This is not surprising. After all, the residents used candles and oil lamps for lighting. In fact, all parts of Roman cities were at a high risk for fires. This greatly bothered the first emperor, Augustus (reigned 30 BC – AD 14). So he introduced a solution that can still be found in every modern city. It was the first professional firefighting brigade. He organized about 7,000 firemen. People called them "watchmen." They were mostly freedmen, formerly enslaved men who had gained their

9

freedom. The government paid them regular salaries.

To put out fires, the watchmen often carried water in huge pottery jars, along with axes, on horse-drawn wagons to the blaze. Over time they also crafted hand-operated pumps and leather hoses. These allowed them to draw water from public fountains.

Besides being prone to fires, the apartments had no kitchens. As a result, many residents dined out most of the time. This inspired another Roman institution that is also common today. Back then, most city folk could not afford to go to fancy, pricey restaurants for every meal. Hence, there was a need for inexpensive "fast food."

When you need to eat on the go, or when you're out and about, you might grab a quick burger at your favorite fast-food joint. The Romans had their own places to get a quick bite to eat. Such fare was available at several different kinds of shops. One consisted of small cookshops called *thermopolii*. At least one could be found on every block. It served hot sausages and other cooked meats along with cheese, bread, cake, olives, and figs and other fruit. Although cookshops served wine as well, people could find a wider variety of wine at bars known as *popinae*. Because they specialized in drink, a *popina*'s food choices were more limited than those in the cookshops. Fast food and drink could also be found at taverns, or *taberna*. They offered an added feature—a bed for the night.

For some city-dwellers even fast food was sometimes too costly. Augustus and other early emperors recognized the challenge of feeding the city's poor. The worry was that those who lacked food might stage protests. That could lead to riots or even rebellion. To avoid such disorders, leaders turned to social welfare. Today social welfare takes the form of food stamps and other government programs that aid people in need. The Roman version consisted of handouts of free sacks of grain in the cities. People took the grain to a baker, and they converted it to bread.

FACT

Little "fast-food" shops were widely popular in Roman cities. More than 200 of them have been found in the ruins of the small city of Pompeii. So there must have been thousands of them in the far larger city of Rome.

The snack bar in Pompeii run by a citizen named Vetutius Placidus was largely preserved by volcanic debris from Mt. Vesuvius's AD 79 eruption, which entombed the town. The circular holes built into the bar were for large jars that once held food or wine.

THE SPREAD OF NEWS AND KNOWLEDGE

Where do you look to find out what's going on in your city? Roman culture produced yet another item in common use today. Newspapers are a regular part of today's life. In addition to news, they provide sports scores, birth and death notices, and much more. The Romans created the model for what became the newspaper. They called it *Acta Diurna,* meaning "daily acts." It consisted of a daily posting. No paper, as we now know it, was involved. Rather, the words were carved on stone walls or tablets. Such a posting informed the public about the latest happenings. Included were the dates of upcoming gladiator bouts, for example. New laws were listed, as were birth and death notices. There were even ancient versions of horoscopes.

Today, when you want to find other information, you may need to look beyond the newspaper. This was the same for the Romans. More permanent knowledge was recorded in books. Although the Romans did not invent them, they did introduce the most common kind used today—the bound book. The Egyptians, Greeks, and other earlier peoples wrote on a sort of paper called papyrus. It was made from a plant. They wound the sheets into a scroll. This form of book was fragile and wore out quickly.

In the first century, the Romans began making more durable bound books. The pages were sometimes made of papyrus. But over time vellum became more common. Vellum was a parchment made from the skin of sheep, goats, or cattle. A bookmaker stitched the pages to a wooden spine. Then he added sturdy front and back covers. The finished book was called a *codex*. Because Roman books were handmade, they tended to be fairly costly. So well-to-do people were the only ones who could afford to own more than one or two.

TRYING TO KEEP WARM

Today, we have many ways to stay warm during cold weather. We have warm socks, hot baths, and built-in heating systems. Wealthy Romans also benefited from such ways to keep warm.

In fact, the Romans originally came up with the idea for built-in heat. A luxury then, today such systems are standard in nearly all homes. Less well-to-do Romans heated their apartments using braziers. These were metal pots for burning wood. They produced smoke and fumes and had to be refilled often. In contrast, many wealthier homes used a device called a hypocaust. It was invented by a clever merchant, Gaius Sergius Orata, and introduced in about 100 BC. It required a cellar about 3 feet (1 m) tall beneath the house. A brick-lined duct, or channel, connected the cellar to a furnace located outside the building. Enslaved people operated the furnace, which burned wood. The heat produced traveled through the

The remains of a hypocaust are visible in an excavated building in northern Cyprus, dating from the island's Roman period. The rows of vertical posts were in the subfloor, where warm air circulated and heated the room above.

duct and into the cellar. Because heat rises, the house's floors got warmer, which, in turn, heated up the rooms.

Roman bathhouses also used hypocausts. Those devices heated the water and interior spaces. All Roman citizens, wealthy and poor, could and did attend the baths. Another way all Romans kept warm was by wearing socks. Some earlier peoples, including the Greeks, wore socks. But the Romans were first to use well-made, affordable ones on an empire-wide scale. Today, people worldwide benefit from the countless ideas and customs the Romans either invented or improved upon.

THE JULIAN CALENDAR

The calendar used in most nations today originated in ancient Rome. For a long time the Romans used a calendar based on the moon's cycles. It had twelve months. Several of the month's names are still in use today. For instance, the Roman Januarius is now called January, and Aprilis is now April. One problem was that the moon's cycles were a little shorter than a solar year. (That is how long it takes Earth to circle the sun.) It was a small difference. But over time it added up. Eventually, the lunar calendar was three months ahead of the solar year. The famous general and statesman Julius Caesar decided to reform this system. At his direction, the year 46 BC had 445 days. After that each year had 365 days. He said every few years an extra day should be added to correct for minor errors. Such years are now called leap years. With a few minor changes, this so-called Julian calendar remains in use today.

CHAPTER 2

THE GREATEST PREMODERN BUILDERS

Today, vast networks of roads and bridges connect cities and countries. Meanwhile, those cities are filled with large-scale buildings. Most utilize enormous amounts of concrete. Maybe you or a friend lives in an apartment building that rises to multiple floors with many rooms. You can visit cities with busy shopping centers. Imagine a day out and about, seeing a movie or a play with friends. Or perhaps watching football in a huge stadium with tens of thousands of fans is more your style.

None of these things are new. The Romans were the first to create large cities connected by vast road networks. They had apartment buildings. They were also the first to use concrete on a big scale. Even today's enormous stadiums and racetracks for athletes, horses, and race cars are not new. The Romans built giant stadiums where gladiators fought, often to the death. Roman stadiums also featured exciting animal shows. The Romans built gigantic structures called circuses, where chariots raced. All of these things made the Romans the greatest of all premodern builders.

Today a lot of architecture and buildings were inspired by the Romans. Yet the Roman builders were rarely original or inventive. They frequently borrowed architectural styles from others. Most often the Romans copied the Greeks and a fellow Italian people, the Etruscans. In many ways, Roman temples looked similar to Greek temples. This is because Roman builders saw Greek temple architecture as noble-looking. So they copied it. The Romans also borrowed the idea of racetracks from the Greeks.

However, the way the Romans applied foreign ideas and styles set them apart. In particular, they erected structures on a far larger scale than anyone before them. Their bathhouses held hundreds of people at once. Many Roman stadiums had room for tens of thousands. And

The famous Colosseum was Rome's largest amphitheater for staging gladiator fights and other public entertainments. It was opened by the emperor Titus (reigned 79 to 81).

the largest Roman racetrack, the Circus Maximus, seated well over 100,000 cheering fans—just like Churchill Downs, a current horse track in Louisville, Kentucky. Each year up to 170,000 excited fans crowd into that racetrack to watch the Kentucky Derby.

COLOSSAL CURVES IN CONSTRUCTION

Most of those huge Roman structures featured a few basic ideas, styles, and kinds of building materials. Today, when you see a stone bridge with beautiful arcs, it's not just for looks! It's also an old and strong design.

The two most common Roman architectural innovations were the arch and vault. Most experts believe the Romans borrowed the arch from the Etruscans. A single arch could support a great amount of weight. Today, builders use arches for the same reason. Now that familiar shape can be seen in thousands of bridges around the world. The enormous arches support the weight of the many

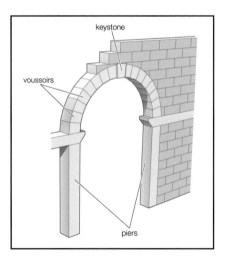

A Roman arch had three basic parts. It had two upright supports called piers. Some piers were solid columns. Others were stacks of stone blocks. An arch also had a wedge-shaped stone, the voussoir (voo-SWAR). Rows of voussoirs curved inward from the tops of the piers. They met at the arch's third basic part, a single central block called the keystone.

cars, trucks, and people that cross them every day.

Think of huge cathedrals such as Notre Dame in Paris with high, curved ceilings. Somehow, these huge structures have to support their own weight. What keeps them from collapsing? The answer is partly in that curved ceiling. It's called a vault. Stones of vaults were aligned in the same manner as those in an arch. The Romans used several kinds of vaults. Perhaps the most common was the barrel vault, which could support a lot of weight. It was a long corridor that featured a curved ceiling running along its length. Examples of Roman barrel vaults still survive. Some are in the ruins of the famous amphitheater, the Colosseum, in Rome. When spectators entered the Colosseum, they walked through large barrel-vaulted corridors to reach the structure's seating sections. Barrel vaults were also used in later ages, such as in those huge cathedrals, in order to support their upper sections. Another stunning example is the Kimbell Art Museum in Fort Worth, Texas. Completed in 1972, it features five barrel-vaulted galleries.

In other large buildings today, we simply use strong materials, such as concrete. The Romans were one of the first to use concrete. Other common building materials they used included marble and a kind of limestone called travertine. They also used compressed volcanic ash and wood. However, none of those substances proved as strong and durable as concrete. The Romans first learned how to make it around 300 BC. It consisted of a mix of sand and cement composed of volcanic ash and lime mortar. When dry, Roman concrete was rock-solid. The builders usually applied it in layers. Sometimes they used gravel between the concrete layers, a method that is still being used.

HIGH WATER: AQUEDUCTS AND BRIDGES

How much harder would your life be if you didn't have water in your home? Likewise, how much harder would it be to get around if we didn't have an easy way across rivers? Just as we have water pipes and bridges today, the Romans found effective ways to bring water to cities and the ability to cross rivers.

Many Roman building projects had certain features in common. The same basic ideas, styles, and materials were used. Builders commonly erected several arches beside one another. This was done when the structure they wanted to hold up was too big or long for one arch to support. Such a graceful row of arches is called an arcade. Arcades could also be stacked on top of one another. Rows and stacks of arches appear throughout the Colosseum's remains. Roman amphitheaters used them extensively. Parts of circuses also featured various single arches and arcades. These giant racetracks could be as long as six modern football fields.

Romans used arcades to support water channels called aqueducts. Aqueducts served the same purpose that a town's water systems do today. Roman towns required fresh water for drinking and bathing. But lakes and other water sources were sometimes miles away. Aqueducts carried the water into the towns. Most sections of these aqueducts were located underground. But in certain areas they ran above ground. There, arcades, both singly and in stacks, were needed to hold them up.

These water systems were extremely well built. Incredibly, a few are still in use after thousands of years. One example is the aqueduct in Segovia, in northern Spain. Its arcade is 95 feet (29 m) tall and stretches for 2,388 feet (728 m).

The Romans also used arches and arcades in their bridges over rivers. Here, instead of water channels, the arches supported roadways for wagons, horses, and people. Before installing a bridge's lower parts, some of the water had to be briefly removed. In the midst of the river, engineers built a big wooden box. It was open at the top. Then they pumped the water out of the box. After a while the ground inside the box dried out. At that point the builders laid in the bridge's massive foundation. After adding a long arcade on top of it, they removed the box, letting the water flow naturally. Finally, they built the roadway atop the arcade. Several Roman bridges remain in use today, including the Pons Fabricius in Rome.

They were so well built that they easily carry the weight of modern trucks, cars, and buses. Their strength and quality inspired today's builders. So, many stone bridges erected in the modern era look almost identical to the ancient Roman ones.

ON THE OPEN ROMAN ROAD

We take modern roads for granted. Most of us probably don't have to worry about how we're going to travel over rocky hills, through thick forests, or across endless stretches of prairie. But with the help of modern equipment, we've connected nearly everything with roads!

Even without such equipment, the Romans built an impressive system of roads. These roads made their vast empire possible to carve out and rule. Roads allowed the Romans to ship their soldiers, merchants, and way of life to distant lands. The roads also made it easier to control the places they conquered. Over time new towns sprouted up along the roads. Several of them later became densely populated European cities.

The first step in building a new road was to lay out the route. Surveyors did this using simple sighting tools. One, called a *groma*, was very similar to a modern surveyor's cross. As they made their way through the countryside, they set up posts at intervals. These showed gangs of workers where to clear the land and dig trenches. Those trenches would hold the new roadbed.

Some of the workers were free men who lived in nearby villages and towns. Some earned salaries for their labor. Others traded the work for eliminating part of their tax burden. It was also common for Roman soldiers to help build roads. Enslaved people were rarely used. This was partly because feeding and housing them was very expensive. It cost almost as much as paying free men. Also, the free men were easier to manage because they did not require guards.

After digging the trenches, workers laid in the roadbed's bottom layer. It consisted of small- to medium-sized rocks mixed with clay. This created a sturdier base than ordinary dirt. It ensured that the road would not sag under the weight of pack animals, wagons, and other heavy traffic. Atop that initial layer, the workers installed the road's surface. Sometimes it was composed of coarse gravel. Other times it consisted of paving stones. In fact, thousands of miles of Roman roads were paved with these stones.

Did you ever notice that roads are constructed so the middle section sits slightly higher than the outer edges? This technique, called cambering, was used by the Romans. In a cambered road, the rainwater runs off toward the sides so no puddles form in the road. Roman road-builders also borrowed an idea from the Greeks and Etruscans. It consisted of rows of narrow ruts carved into the road's surface. These guided the wheels of wagons and chariots, which kept them from skidding.

FACT

One of several ancient Roman words for a road was *via*. It specifically referred to a road wide enough for two wagons to pass each other. The most famous example was the Via Appia, or Appian Way. It ran south from Rome for 370 miles (595 kilometers).

Large sections of the Via Appia have survived. In addition to its importance for travelers and traders, well-to-do Roman families often lined the road with tombs of deceased relatives.

ROME'S PERMANENT STAMP

Imagine if you took a long road trip and there were no signs, rest stops, gas stations, restaurants, or motels. This idea didn't appeal to Roman travelers any more than it does to today's travelers! And it often took Romans several days to go from one city to another. So road-builders included roadside services.

The Roman version of road signs was milestones. These carved stone slabs stood at intervals of one mile. (A Roman mile was slightly shorter than a modern mile.) Also, posting stations sat at intervals along the Roman roads. These were comparable to gas stations. A mail carrier, merchant, or other traveler could obtain a fresh horse at a posting station. He or she could also get food and drink there. For those travelers who wanted a bed for the night, inns existed along the roads. The remains of one of those inns was found in the twentieth century in Austria. It was originally 70 feet (21 m) long, 43 feet (13 m) wide, and two stories tall. Besides bed chambers, it had a roomy dining area. It also featured a stable for the traveler's animals and a repair shop for wagons.

The Roman road system eventually covered most of Europe. When the Roman Empire was in decline, those highways remained. People continued to use them in medieval and early modern times. A few are still in use today. Others lie beneath modern roads built directly on top of them. Thus, many of the routes Roman surveyors laid out long ago are still intact.

Post-Roman societies also inherited Roman ruins spread across Europe. They included stadiums, racetracks, temples, palaces, and other large-scale structures. Medieval and early modern builders copied many of their features. They also continued to employ numerous Roman construction methods. Only in the last century and a half did builders manage to surpass their Roman forebears.

Roman milestones could be found throughout the Roman road system. Initially they were made of expensive types of stone, such as marble or granite. But over time concrete became the material of choice for these markers.

Yet Roman influences remain. Stadiums and racetracks retain the basic shapes of the Roman versions. Levi's Stadium, erected in San Clara, California, in 2014, was even modeled directly on Roman amphitheaters. Roman engineers and builders clearly left a permanent stamp on human civilization.

The "Bordeaux Itinerary," also known as the "Bordeaux Anonymous" (because the identity of its author remains unknown), is the oldest known Christian road guide. It recounts a religious pilgrim's journey from France to the Holy Land in Palestine (now Israel) in the 300s.

THE BORDEAUX ITINERARY

One of the many services that travelers in late Roman times enjoyed were guidebooks. They called them "itineraries." They were not thick, bound books. Rather, they had only a few pages, like modern pamphlets. But like today's guidebooks they showed the locations of towns along the roads. They also indicated where various services could be found. Most of those ancient books no longer exist. But a few have survived. One dates from the early 300s. It was made specially for Roman Christian travelers. Today the author is often referred to as the Bordeaux Pilgrim. This is because he lived in what is now the French town of Bordeaux. On occasion, he and other Roman Christians visited the Holy Land—now Israel. To get there they had to journey through the vast Roman realm. The trip took months. So they needed places to stay overnight. The Bordeaux Itinerary shows where numerous inns and posting stations were located.

CHAPTER 3

ENTERTAINING COMBAT: THE GLADIATORS

Muscular professional wrestlers clash as thousands of fans cheer. Opposing football players put on helmets and other protective gear. They do battle in huge stadiums while millions watch on television. Also various TV shows have restaged the combats between ancient gladiators. All of these contests have something in common. Namely, they are widely popular forms of entertainment.

These and other modern examples of mock combat share a second trait. They all echo contests in ancient Rome. The Roman versions were different in one way, however. Rather than mock combats, they were real fights to the death. Those bloody bouts between gladiators in Roman stadiums have become familiar images. Besides

TV shows, many big-budget movies have depicted them, attracting enormous audiences. Public interest in such spectacles—whether mock or real—links ancient Rome to modern society.

FROM PRIVATE RITUAL TO PUBLIC SHOW

College football is one of several modern sports that began as a way to channel violence off of college campuses into something more productive. Over time, it grew into a widely popular sport. The way these big public spectacles developed from small, private events is modeled in the same way as many Roman forms of entertainment.

Of course, combat between gladiators was hugely popular in Rome. But it was not the only kind of large-scale entertainment the Romans enjoyed. They also loved

In a modern reenactment, a two-horse chariot, called a *biga* in Latin, is about to be raced in a Roman circus. The chariots employed in those races came in many sizes and types. A four-horse version was known as a *quadriga*.

watching animals fight animals and people fight animals. In addition, audiences flocked to dangerous chariot races. These were staged in the giant racetracks called circuses. Charioteers were frequently maimed or killed.

Yet for sheer brutality, none of the public shows compared to the gladiator combats. It might have been due to a hearty respect for heroic ancestors. These fights actually began as a way to honor dead relatives. Early in Rome's history, the passing of an important man was a solemn event. Simple expressions of grief were not enough to honor him. His family members felt they had a duty to shed blood in his memory.

His family members felt they had a duty to shed blood in his memory.

At first this took place in a ritual performed beside his tomb. The family dragged in and killed an enslaved person or war prisoner. In time, this custom became more elaborate. The family gave weapons to two slaves and forced them to fight to the death. At first only family members witnessed such combat. But later guests were invited.

The ceremony continued to expand. In 200 BC, twenty-five pairs of fighters performed at a nobleman's funeral. The number of fighters—now known as gladiators—kept increasing. Also, it became customary to allow members of the public to watch. This proved a crucial turning point. Although still a funeral ritual, an increasing number of people found it entertaining. By the first century BC, the entertainment aspect had become most important. From then on, thousands of Romans eagerly attended public shows involving gladiators.

CHOOSING AND TRAINING GLADIATORS

Modern football and other popular sports have training camps. The camps carry on an ancient tradition of strict, relentless training to gain the proper skills. However, they are not as harsh as the ones Roman gladiators had to participate in. In the beginning, the funeral fighters had been enslaved people and war prisoners. That custom continued in later times. At the peak of popularity, most gladiators were not free. They had no rights. Treated as property, they were often bought and sold. Some masters forced them to fight in the public games. If one of those gladiators survived all his bouts, his master might free him. But that scenario was the exception to the rule. Free or not, many gladiators became skilled professionals who won many of their fights.

Not all gladiators were enslaved, however. A handful of them were free citizens who volunteered to fight. Some did so for money. The men who staged the spectacles sometimes offered cash prizes to fighters who frequently won. Other volunteers enjoyed the challenge of fighting for their lives. Still others did it in hopes of impressing women.

No matter how someone became a gladiator, he had to be trained. To that end, a number of gladiator schools arose. They were called *ludi*. The capital city of Rome had three ludi that taught men how to fight. The trainees followed strict rules. Harsh punishments awaited those who broke them. They lived in small brick-lined cells inside the ludus. Each cell was only a few feet wide and often had no windows. Despite these discomforts, the trainees learned everything about weapons and became skilled warriors.

FACT

The largest Roman gladiator school was the Ludus Magnus. It was located near the Colosseum, Rome's most splendid amphitheater. An underground tunnel connected the school and Colosseum. The gladiators used that passage to enter and exit. Its ruins still survive.

THE OPENING CEREMONY

Stadium seats are filled. Fans cheer for their favorite team. Athletes line up. In a show of ceremony, everything pauses as the national anthem is sung. Compare this familiar event to one in which large, enthusiastic crowds gathered around the open oval space at the center of a stadium, such as the Colosseum. Finally the trainees were ready to fight in the arena, and the crowd wanted to be entertained. The managers of these exhibitions did not disappoint them.

The show began with a splendid parade, in some ways not unlike a Super Bowl halftime show. The Romans called it a *pompa*. In an impressive display, the gladiators marched into the arena. With them were a number of musicians. They played a lively fanfare on their flutes and trumpets and marchers beat on their drums. There were also acrobats, jugglers, and other performers. The spectators applauded to signal their approval.

Following the opening ceremony, these performers left the arena. Then, at a given signal, the gladiators faced the highest ranking official present. It might be a military general or a senator. Or occasionally, it might be an emperor.

All of the fighters now departed the arena except for those whose bout was the first on that day's card. These men were not alone, however. Standing nearby were two referees who could stop the contest at any time. A referee could let the fighters take a brief rest. He could also use a stick to beat a fighter who had broken a rule.

DIFFERENT KINDS OF GLADIATORS

Modern pro wrestlers put on intense displays grappling with opponents. They act tough and fierce. But there are no modern sports figures who are the exact equivalents of Roman gladiators. After all, modern pro wrestlers don't actually try to kill each other. Yet for entertainment value, many of today's wrestlers dress and act like ancient warriors.

A gladiator fight was vigorous and frequently bloody. The way these opponents fought depended on their weapons and armor. The Roman public games featured several different kinds of gladiators. Each kind employed distinct armor and weapons. For instance, a *retiarius* carried a large net. That earned him the nickname "net man." He also wielded a three-pronged spear and wore no armor. His chief tactic was to trap his adversary in the net and then stab him with the spear.

Often paired with a net man was a gladiator called a *murmillo*. The latter was armed with a sword and a large shield. He also had a metal helmet and armor that covered his sword arm. The word *murmillo* means "fish man." He was so named because his helmet bore a fish-shaped crest.

A third type of gladiator, the Thracian, fought bare-

chested. But his legs were well protected. Strips of leather wound around his thighs and metal bands, called greaves, encircled his lower legs. He carried a short, curved sword and a small, round shield.

Over time numerous other types of gladiators appeared in Roman arenas. Each had a certain specialty that audiences enjoyed. One, the *equite*, rode a horse. He had a sword and a long spear. Another kind of mounted fighter attacked his opponent with a lasso, like that wielded by American cowboys. Apparently he tossed the rope, hoping to either trip or choke his adversary.

One type of gladiator used horses in a different way. He fought from a chariot drawn by those steeds.

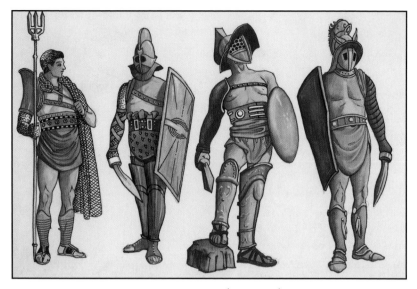

There were numerous kinds of gladiators including (left to right) a retiarius, or "net man"; a thrax (or thraex), meaning "Thracian"; a samnite; and a secutor.

Sometimes one gladiator opposed another. But other times the fighter in the vehicle was paired with a fighter on foot. In that case, the charioteer tried to run over his opponent. That could backfire, however. If the gladiator managed to dodge the chariot, he could circle back. Then he could attack the charioteer from behind.

More unusual were gladiators who fought with two swords, one in each hand. Perhaps most bizarre of all were fighters who wore helmets with no eyeholes. Thus, they were unable to see each other. For the audience they must have provided a sort of comic relief. Yet they still swung swords in an effort to kill each other. Their strategy and moves remain unclear. But apparently they were still very entertaining for an eager audience.

POSSIBLE OUTCOMES

Many reality TV contests today allow the audience to vote for their favorite singer or dancer. The viewers can choose who stays and who must leave. Never knowing who'll get to stay is part of the excitement and suspense! More certain were the outcomes of the bouts the gladiators fought. One of the more common outcomes was when one fighter killed the other. A gladiator could also win by seriously wounding his adversary.

A fallen, injured gladiator was forbidden from touching his weapon again. If he broke that rule, the show's manager could order his instant death. The fallen fighter was allowed to raise a single finger. Doing so was a request that his life be spared. The manager then decided whether or not to grant that request.

Sometimes the manager asked the crowd to weigh in. Many people think a thumbs-up means "let him live." Also, a thumbs-down signals "kill him." But most experts tell us this is incorrect. Some believe the thumbs-down gesture means "weapons down." The losing fighter was thereby spared. How the onlookers signaled his death is unclear. They may have pointed their thumbs at their chests. This would signify a sword thrust to the heart. What we do know is that the crowd's decision had much more fatal outcomes than TV voting today!

Such crowd reactions show how much the Romans enjoyed gladiator fights. Yet they eventually banned them. In the 300s, Roman Christians rose to power. They viewed the gladiator bouts as murder. So Christian emperors banned these shows.

The idea of exciting contests between warriors never died, however. In medieval times armored knights jousted in mock battles. Similarly, all sorts of pretend combats thrive in modern sports and movies. Thus, the bloody Roman version is gone. But its imitators remain alive and well.

FACT

Most Hollywood movies have depicted gladiators inaccurately. One of the few exceptions came out in 1954. Titled *Demetrius and the Gladiators,* it contains a realistic recreation of the pompa. Its gladiator battles are also some of the best ever filmed.

Popular modern illustrator Angus McBride, who specializes in bringing the ancient world to life, painted the pompa, the colorful parade that preceded a program of gladiator fights.

Domitian was Titus's younger brother. As emperor (from 81 to 96), Domitian frequently sponsored public games and was a huge fan of chariot racing.

WOMEN WHO FOUGHT AS GLADIATORS

Roman gladiators were overwhelmingly men. However, a small number of them were female. The emperor Domitian (reigned 81-96) was a big fan of their bouts. He especially liked it when they fought male dwarfs. The "stage names" of a few of these female fighters have survived. One called herself Achillia. That was the feminine form of Achilles, a famous Greek hero. Another woman gladiator used the name Amazonia. This referred to the Amazons, a legendary tribe of female warriors. Roman society frowned on women who took part in public displays. Also, most Romans disliked it when women did so-called "men's jobs." So female gladiators were generally viewed as socially unacceptable. The emperor Septimius Severus (reigned 193-211) certainly felt that way. He banned women from becoming gladiators.

CHAPTER 4

ANIMAL SHOWS FOR EVERYONE

Each year millions of people worldwide attend shows featuring animals. Circuses include animal acts. Elephants, tigers, and all sorts of other beasts do amazing tricks. In the United States, Canada, and Mexico, rodeos are also popular. People ride and rope horses and bulls in front of cheering crowds. Laws prohibit injuring or killing creatures in circuses and rodeos. But no such rules govern other popular activities involving animals. In Spain, for example, each year thousands of bulls die during bullfights. Also, thousands of big-game hunters from around the globe annually visit Africa. They shoot many thousands of zebras, antelopes, rhinos, and other wild animals.

These and other activities involving animals have varied origins. One factor links them all, however. They echo the huge animal shows of ancient Rome. First, Roman hunters tracked down and captured the beasts. They then transported them to Roman cities for the public spectacles. Like gladiator fights, these were mainly staged in amphitheaters. However, they sometimes took place in the giant racetracks called circuses. Smaller animal shows were even held in town squares.

These shows were incredibly popular. The Romans were both dependent upon and fascinated by animals. They used them for transportation and food. They also kept them as pets. In addition, various creatures became offerings to the gods.

No other type of Roman spectacle featured as many variations as animal shows. One consisted of so-called

Events of modern rodeos, such as roping a bull, are astoundingly similar to several events performed by arena hunters in animal games staged in Roman amphitheaters.

hunts. In them, men, and sometimes women, fought and killed various animals. In a second kind of show, animals battled other animals. A third variation witnessed the maiming and death of prisoners by wild beasts. (When the government persecuted early Christians, some of the Christians met this fate.) Finally, parts of some shows were devoted to trained animals performing tricks. In a sense, therefore, there were animal shows for everyone.

TWO KINDS OF HUNTERS

Where do circus and zoo animals come from? Today, these animals are often born in captivity or were injured and rescued from the wild. Sometimes this takes teams of people and lots of money to accomplish. Similarly, supplying the animals for the ancient Romans' large-scale displays was itself a big operation. Capturing the creatures took thousands of hunters and their support crews. It was extremely expensive. So only the government and a few wealthy people could afford it.

The hunters sought their prey in all corners of the known world. Leopards and lions came from Africa and Syria. Tigers came from India, and bears came from Africa and central Europe. Elephants were captured in both Africa and India. The hunters found crocodiles in Egypt and horses in Spain. Methods of capture varied widely. Some beasts fell into pits the hunters dug. In other cases, people chased the animals into big nets or cages. Still others got caught in leg traps. Some of those same capture methods are still used today in parts of the world.

When the captured beasts reached a city, they were held in cages. They were also separated into groups. Those in one group were to be killed in arenas. Others would be trained to amuse audiences. The animals chosen to die were part of shows called hunts. The fighters who killed them were known as *venatores*, or hunters. They were different from the professional hunters who captured the animals. Like gladiators, most arena hunters were initially enslaved people. A few were free-men volunteers. They attended a ludus that specialized in training arena hunters.

An ancient Roman relief sculpture shows arena hunters battling wild animals. One common Latin name for these fighters was *bestiarius*, translating roughly as "beast-fighter" or "beast-master."

VAST NUMBERS OF ANIMALS SLAIN

While animals are not often killed for sport today, there are a few exceptions. Bullfights or big-game hunts still result in the deaths of thousands of animals. In ancient Roman arenas, animal fights took on many forms.

In a showdown between an animal and arena hunter, the venator simply stalked, fought, and killed it. Arena hunters did this with a variety of weapons. One was a sturdy spear with an iron tip. Others included clubs, swords, daggers, and bows and arrows.

These animal fighters also used diverse attack methods. Hunters armed with bows and arrows fired several shots from a distance. When the beast was wounded and weak enough, the hunter moved in and finished it off with a sword or club. Other arena hunters were like modern bullfighters. They squared off with bulls or other beasts and tried to stab them using swords or spears. Another approach resembled a popular modern rodeo event. In it, a hunter on horseback circled the prey. When the time was right, the hunter leaped off the horse.

FACT

In AD 107, the emperor Trajan held games that included animal shows. The games lasted 123 days and modern historians estimate that at least 11,000 beasts were killed. Among them were lions, elephants, hyenas, hippos, and giraffes.

He landed on the animal and wrestled it to the ground. Then he killed it, unless it killed him first. A number of venatores did meet grisly deaths in the course of their jobs.

Some arena hunters managed to survive many fights. Such frequent winners were highly popular with the public. One named Carpophorus became famous in the first century. The Roman poet Martial praised him in verse. Like gladiators who often won, a successful venator might collect a lot of prize money. If he was enslaved, he could use the money to buy his freedom.

Over time, a large number of animals were slain by fighters like Carpophorus. The death toll was greatest during special celebrations. One example was when the Colosseum was completed in AD 80. The emperor Titus wanted to celebrate its grand opening. So he announced 100 days of public games. An estimated 9,000 animals died in the new arena in that single period.

TRAINED ANIMAL ACTS

People today enjoy observing exotic, wild creatures up close in zoos. Zoos provide a chance to see and learn about animals we'd otherwise never get to see. Likewise, the Romans enjoyed trained animal shows. No animals were killed during these shows like in the animal fights. In a way, the shows served the same purpose as modern zoos.

Performing monkeys were widely popular, for example. Surviving ancient writings describe how trainers often dressed them like soldiers. Some rode in mini-chariots pulled by goats. Lions were also a big attraction. Trainers taught at least one lion to hold a rabbit in its jaws without hurting it. Meanwhile, trained bears climbed up and down tall poles.

Dogs, the Romans' favorite pet, also performed. The first-century Greek writer Plutarch described some of their antics. One talented pooch, he said, pretended to eat food containing poison. The creature seemed to become distressed. It rolled around on the ground and then lay still, as if dead. Suddenly, however, it sprang back to life and enjoyed the audience's applause and cheers.

The Romans' favorite trained animal by far was the elephant. They nicknamed elephants "Lucanian cows." Several ancient writers described performing elephants. In one such act, 12 of them—six males and six females—entered the arena. They walked to tables set with dinner plates, cups, and food. The huge creatures then pretended to eat and drink like people. Other elephants danced to music supplied by musicians.

The Romans' fascination with elephants is easy to understand. Like people today, they sensed that these beasts are unusually intelligent. A number of incidents confirmed this fact to Roman observers. Maybe the most moving one involved an elephant that was learning a new trick. It tried hard but could not quite master it. In response, the trainer whipped it. Late that night, someone saw something remarkable in the creature's pen. The elephant was practicing the trick over and over, trying to get it right.

ANIMAL SHOWS IN LATER AGES

Although circuses are no longer as popular in some areas as they once were, we still enjoy animal acts in other ways. We enjoy movies and TV shows featuring clever dogs and bonds between humans and animals. The same seems true for the Romans and their animal acts.

The animal shows remained popular for the rest of Rome's history. Only when the empire fell apart in the late 400s and early 500s did they cease. Yet small remnants of those shows survived in parts of the former empire. The best known example occurred in Spain. There, fights between venatores and bulls remained popular. Over time, these combats evolved into the now famous Spanish bullfights. Indeed, they are still held in circular arenas closely resembling Roman amphitheaters.

Meanwhile, a number of early modern Europeans were inspired by Roman trained-animal acts. One was a retired English army officer, Philip Astley. An expert horseman, he trained his steed to do tricks. In 1768 he staged a show in which he and the horse performed stunts. Soon, he added jugglers and acrobats to the

An 1808 drawing shows a scene from Philip Astley's circus performing near Westminster Bridge, in London. The shape of the arena and overall design of the facility clearly demonstrate the influence of Roman amphitheaters.

program. He created the modern circus.

Following Astley's lead, several more modern circuses formed. The Romans had used that term both for a racetrack and for public games in general. The name soon caught on. Similar to the Romans, some shows added other animals, including elephants. Animal acts of various kinds became standard circus attractions. Today, fascination for animals is as strong as it was in ancient Rome.

Today, fascination for animals is as strong as it was in ancient Rome.

A Roman dish dating from about 250 BC bears an image of a war elephant. The Romans first encountered elephants in 280 BC during a battle with the Greek general Pyrrhus. In time, elephants became a favorite animal in Rome's wild beast shows.

HIGH DRAMA IN THE ARENA

The Romans saw elephants for the first time in about 280 BC. Later, those huge beasts appeared regularly in public games and shows. Multiple Roman writers mentioned a dramatic incident that occurred at one of those events. In 55 BC a wealthy military general named Pompey sponsored an arena hunt. He shipped in several elephants for the show. Following tradition, the venatores began attacking the creatures. They were in for a surprise, however. One elephant fought back valiantly. It grabbed their shields and hurled them away. Over time it was badly wounded. Though now unable to stand, it charged the hunters on its knees. Meanwhile, the other elephants faced the audience. The beasts moaned and gestured as if pleading for mercy. Many spectators were genuinely moved. They cried out for the remaining elephants to be spared. When this didn't work, the crowd yelled curses at Pompey. Pompey's plan to boost his popularity by killing elephants had backfired.

INHERITING THE ROMAN WAY OF WAR

It was still dark in the early morning of January 17, 1991. Iraq's largest city, Baghdad, was quiet. Most of its residents were sleeping. Suddenly the skies lit up. Enormous bombs exploded in key areas across the city. It was the opening action of the Gulf War. Iraq had recently invaded its neighbor, the tiny nation of Kuwait. Now the United States and its allies had come to free Kuwait. They went on to achieve that goal in only a few months.

The attack that began on January 17 lasted weeks. Iraq's armed forces were both shocked and scared. That was indeed the military's intent. People began to call it "shock and awe." It was a new name for a common modern military tactic. It aims to employ overwhelming power in a grand display of force. Almost always it damages an enemy's will to fight. This tactic is often used by large, powerful Western, or European-based, nations. It is part of a bigger concept known as "total war." In it, a country throws all its resources into a conflict. The enemy nation is brutally beaten down until it is utterly defeated. It must surrender or be destroyed.

Modern nations borrowed both shock and awe and total war from ancient Rome. The Greeks came up with these ideas and used them on a small scale. Then Rome conquered the Greek lands. In the process, it absorbed Greek military concepts. The Romans expanded and perfected shock and awe and total war. They used them repeatedly to fashion their vast and mighty empire. Eventually, they passed their distinct ideas about war on to the modern world.

U.S. bombs light up the sky above Baghdad, Iraq, during the evening of January 18, 1991, at the start of the first Gulf War. Labeled "shock and awe" by reporters, this sort of sudden, overwhelming attack continues a tradition begun long ago by Greek and Roman armies.

IN AWE OF THE GREEKS

Before Rome rose to power, the Greeks developed a new form of warfare. Greek foot soldiers were called hoplites. They wore heavy protective armor. Hence, they were the first "heavy infantry," now a common term. Using spears and swords, the hoplites fought in a special formation. They called it a phalanx. It consisted of several lines of soldiers, one behind another. The entire formation marched forward as a block. In a later version, a mass of spear points stuck out from the front. It was one of the most lethal fighting machines in the world. It easily mowed down ordinary armies. The Greeks used it to wage total war on their enemies.

In the late 300s BC Greek phalanxes invaded Persia. They were led by Alexander the Great. The Persian Empire was then the largest in history. It covered most of the Middle East and included dozens of native peoples. Alexander's armies brought Persia to its knees in only a decade. No city or people escaped him as he waged total war.

People across southern Europe and beyond were awed by the Greek armies. Well before Alexander's campaigns some tried to copy the phalanx. Among them were the

FACT

One standard weapon Roman soldiers carried was a throwing spear called the *pilum*. Each soldier carried two *pila*. While running toward the enemy, he threw the lighter spear. Then he hurled the heavier one. After that he drew and fought with his sword.

early Romans. They organized their own hoplite phalanx. It closely resembled the Greek version. The Roman hoplites were not as successful as the Greek ones, however. Frustrated, in the 300s BC Roman

Modern historical reenactors portray Roman soldiers in a yearly festival that celebrates Rome's founding. The traditional date for that pivotal event is April 21, 753 BC.

leaders abandoned the Greek system. Starting from scratch, they created a new approach to warfare.

PHALANX VS. MANIPLES

The new military system the Romans came up with was based on maniples. The word *maniple* means "handful." In this case, the handfuls were small units of soldiers. Each maniple had between 120 and 160 men. A number of these units approached an enemy army. The maniples could be arranged in numerous ways. Also, at a given signal, soldiers could rapidly fill the gaps between the maniples. In that way, several maniples could transform into unbroken lines of soldiers.

In addition, those lines could be used in rotation. For instance, first the front line of troops attacked. When they grew tired, they retreated in an orderly manner. Then the second line advanced. It could be replaced by a third line. Meanwhile, the soldiers in the first line were resting. If needed, they could launch a new assault. Constant attacks by fresh troops eventually wore the enemy down.

Thus, the new Roman system was highly flexible. In fact, it proved far more flexible than the phalanx. The latter was powerful and hard to penetrate, to be sure. But a phalanx operated efficiently only on flat ground free of obstacles. Moreover, it took much more time and effort to turn in the opposite direction. Thus, if attacked in both the front and rear, its members were in serious trouble. In contrast, the Roman maniples could move swiftly in any direction. They could also operate in rough, hilly terrain. Moreover, they had the potential to surround a phalanx.

The first major test of the two systems occurred in central Greece in 197 BC. In command of the Roman Army was a military general, Titus Flamininus. The Greek king Philip V led a large phalanx. During the battle, about 20 maniples carried out a crucial tactic. They attacked the Greek formation's rear squad. Surrounded, the phalanx fell apart. Its fighters were slaughtered where they stood. The age of the phalanx and Greek military superiority was over.

FACT

Roman soldiers used various formations when attacking an enemy. One of the most effective was the so-called "pig's head." It was shaped like a giant wedge. The pointed front end bore down on and penetrated an enemy line.

Thereafter, Rome's new military system continued to succeed. With it, the Romans swiftly conquered the Greek city-states and kingdoms. The Roman system also continued to evolve. It replaced the maniples with other units. That made the army even more flexible. In time, many other nations fell to Roman steel. By the early 100s, the Roman Empire stretched from England and Spain in the west to Iraq in the east. It contained dozens of defeated foreign peoples.

> In time, many other nations fell to Roman steel.

Flexibility was not the only factor that drove Rome's many victories. Another was discipline. Roman soldiers received a lot of training. They all wielded the same weapons and became highly efficient in their use. Also, officers developed battlefield signals that every fighter knew by heart. In addition, rule-breakers were severely punished. So military rules were rarely broken.

Effective organization was another plus. The army broke down into a series of ranks. It was very similar to the version now used in the United States and other nations. At the top were the military generals. Below them ranged various officers in descending ranks. At the bottom were ordinary foot soldiers, or infantry. Today they are called privates or "grunts." From Roman times until the present, infantry has remained the backbone of Western armies.

Still another factor that made the Roman Army successful was advanced technology. The Greeks and other prior armies had perfected various forms of artillery. Ancient artillery consisted of machines that hurled objects long distances. Catapults flung rocks hundreds of feet, for example. There were also devices that launched giant arrows. The Romans adopted such warfare. They made them even more lethal. With them, they laid siege to and captured towns.

ECHOES OF ROMAN LIFE

The Roman military combined and expertly used all these factors. As a result, Roman armies were widely feared. Often the mere sight of a Roman Army and its war machines was enough to create shock and awe. This caused many enemies to lose the will to fight. But if a people or nation did choose to resist, the Romans did not hesitate to wage total war.

After Rome's decline, Europeans retained much of the Roman way of war. Medieval kingdoms continued to use Roman siege methods and devices. These remained in use right into early modern times. Also, Western armies kept the tradition of shocking and awing an enemy. Along the way, some non-Western armies copied those tactics. From the 1600s on, modern nations employed them in a long series of destructive wars.

These reached their height in the most lethal conflict of all—World War II. It began in Europe in 1939. The German Nazis used shock and awe in their sudden, brutal invasion of Poland. Later, in 1941, the Japanese used the same tactic against the United States. In a sneak attack, Japanese warplanes devastated the U.S. naval base at Pearl Harbor. The war drew in nearly every country in the world. As the Romans had done previously, some nations pursued new weapons technology. This led to the creation of the first atomic bombs. Overall, it was a terrifying ordeal of total war. More than 50 million people died. Millions more were injured. In sheer numbers of casualties, the Roman way of war had reached its peak.

Fortunately, warfare methods have not been Rome's sole legacy to the modern world. More constructive reminders of Roman life surround us. Among the more visible ones, architecture and large road systems stand out. So do fire departments and various forms of entertainment. Newspapers, central heating, and even lesser things, such as warm socks, make our lives easier. In addition, the Romans' language, Latin, survived. Each year millions of high school and college students study it. They learn that English and other modern languages contain countless Latin words.

Perhaps most influential of all has been the Romans' religion. In the 300s, Christianity triumphed in Rome. It replaced earlier Roman faiths. After Rome's fall, Christianity survived. It continued to spread and today is the world's largest religion. Thus, only Rome's government fell all those centuries ago. Numerous aspects of Roman life remain intact. They still shape our daily lives and help to make us who we are.

THE ARMY UNDER AUGUSTUS

The Roman military system changed a great deal over time. During the Roman Empire's long existence, it underwent many reforms. One of the biggest occurred during the reign of the first emperor, Augustus. He ruled from 30 BC to AD 14. Before his time the army was organized into large units called legions. Early legions had between 4,200 and 5,000 soldiers. Augustus increased the size of the legions. Each now had about 5,500 men. That counted cavalry, or mounted fighters. In all, Augustus's army had 28 legions. That created a total of more than 150,000 soldiers. The emperor also overhauled the army's command structure. In charge of each legion was an officer called a legionary legate. Augustus himself chose the legates. The officers who served directly below a legate were called tribunes. There were six in each legion. Below the tribunes were the centurions. That name came from the units they led, known as centuries. Each century had around a hundred men, though at various times it had more or fewer than that.

GLOSSARY

Acta Diurna—daily public announcements painted or carved on walls or tablets

amphitheater—an oval-shaped stadium used for gladiator combats and wild animal shows

aqueduct—a channel that carried water from the water's source into a city

arcade—a row of arches

cambering—making the middle of a road slightly higher than the sides, so that rainwater drains away

circus—a huge Roman racetrack with seating sections for spectators along its sides

codex—a bound book

domus—a house (The plural is also *domus*.)

equites—gladiators who fought on horseback

freedmen—former slaves

greaves—lower-leg protectors for gladiators

hypocaust—a device that circulated heated air beneath a building's floors

insulae—multistoried apartment buildings or blocks

itinerary—a Roman guidebook for travelers

ludi—schools for training gladiators and arena hunters

maniple—a small, Roman battlefield unit

murmillo—a gladiator who fought with a sword and wore a helmet with a fish-shaped crest on it

phalanx—a large block of soldiers who moved in unison

pilum—a Roman throwing spear

pompa—the festive opening ceremony of gladiator bouts and other Roman games

popinae—wine shops or bars

retiarius—a gladiator who fought with a net and three-pronged spear

thermopolii—snack bars that sold cooked meats, bread, cheese, and fruit

travertine—a kind of limestone the Romans often used in building

vellum—a parchment made from the skin of goats, sheep, or other animals

venator—an arena hunter

via—a major Roman road

watchmen—ancient Roman firefighters

ADDITIONAL RESOURCES

Read More

Bell, Samantha S., *Ancient Rome*. Lake Elmo, MN: Focus Readers, 2020.

Howell, Izzi, *The Genius of the Romans*. New York: Crabtree, 2020.

Stokes, Jonathan W., *The Thrifty Guide to Ancient Rome: A Handbook for Time Travelers*. New York: Viking, 2018.

Internet Sites

Great Buildings Online: Roman Colosseum
www.greatbuildings.com/buildings/Roman_Colosseum.html

History Today: Roman Roads
http://www.historytoday.com/logan-thompson/roman-roads

NOVA Online: A Day at the Baths
http://www.pbs.org/wgbh/nova/lostempires/roman/day.html

SELECT BIBLIOGRAPHY

Adkins, Lesley and Roy A. Adkins. *Handbook to Life in Ancient Rome*. New York: Facts On File, 2004.

Aldrete, Gregory S. *Daily Life in the Roman City: Rome, Pompeii, Ostia*. Norman: University of Oklahoma Press, 2009.

Balsdon, J.P.V.D. *Life and Leisure in Ancient Rome*. London: Phoenix, 2002.

Beacham, Richard C. *Spectacle Entertainments of Early Imperial Rome*. New Haven: Yale University Press, 2011.

Brown, Peter. *Through the Eye of a Needle: Wealth, the Fall of Rome, and the Making of Christianity in the West, 350-550 AD*. Princeton: Princeton University Press, 2014.

Cameron, Alan. *Circus Factions: Blues and Greens at Rome and Byzantium*. London: Clarendon Press, 1999.

Casson, Lionel. *Travel in the Ancient World*. Baltimore: The Johns Hopkins University Press, 1994.

Cowell, F.R. *Cicero and the Roman Republic*. New York: Pelican, 1973.

Crawford, Michael. *The Roman Republic*. Waukegan, IL: Fontana, 2011.

Everitt, Anthony. *Augustus: The Life of Rome's First Emperor*. New York: Random House, 2007.

Everitt, Anthony. *Cicero: The Life and Times of Rome's Greatest Politician*. New York: Random House, 2003.

Freeman, Charles. *Egypt, Greece, and Rome: Civilizations of the Ancient Mediterranean*. Oxford, Eng.: Oxford University Press, 2014.

Freeman, Philip. *Oh My Gods: A Modern Retelling of Greek and Roman Myths*. New York: Simon and Schuster, 2012.

Futrell, Alison. *Blood in the Arena: The Spectacle of Roman Power*. Austin: University of Texas Press, 2000.

Gardner, Jane F. *Women in Roman Law and Society*. Indianapolis: Indiana University Press, 1991.

Garnsey, Peter, et al. *The Roman Empire: Economy, Society and Culture*. Berkeley: University of California Press, 2014.

Gibbon, Edward. *The Decline and Fall of the Roman Empire*, ed. David Womersley. 3 vols. New York: Penguin, 2001.

Goldsworthy, Adrian. *The Complete Roman Army*. London: Thames & Hudson, 2011.

Goldsworthy, Adrian. *Roman Warfare*. New York: HarperCollins, 2005.

Grant, Michael. *Gladiators*. New York: Delacorte Press, 1996.

Grant, Michael. *The World of Rome*. New York: New American Library, 1995.

Green, Bernard. *Christianity in Ancient Rome: The First Three Centuries*. Edinburgh: Bloomsbury T. and T. Clark, 2010.

Hamilton, Edith. *The Roman Way*. New York: Norton, 1993.

Harlow, Mary and Lena Larsson Lovén. *Families in the Roman and Late Antique World*. New York: Bloomsbury Academic, 2012.

Haywood, John. *The Penguin Historical Atlas of Ancient Civilizations*. New York: Penguin, 2005.

Hohlfelder, Robert L. *The Maritime World of Ancient Rome*. Ann Arbor: University of Michigan Press, 2008.

Humphrey, John H. *Roman Circuses: Arenas for Chariot Racing*. Berkeley: University of California Press, 1986.

Jones, Mark Wilson. *Principles of Roman Architecture*. New Haven: Yale University Press, 2003.

Kamm, Antony and Abigail Graham. *The Romans: An Introduction*. London: Routledge, 2014.

Kebric, Robert B. *Roman People*. Boston: McGraw-Hill, 2005.

Mattern, Susan P. *The Prince of Medicine: Galen in the Roman Empire*. New York: Oxford University Press, 2013.

Moore, Timothy J. *Roman Theatre*. New York: Cambridge University Press, 2012.

Morford, Mark P.O. and Robert J. Lenardon, *Classical Mythology*. New York: Oxford University Press, 2010.

Oleson, John P. *The Oxford Handbook of Engineering and Technology in the Classical World*. New York: Oxford University Press, 2008.

Petersen, Lauren Hackworth and Patricia Salzman-Mitchell. *Mothering and Motherhood in Ancient Greece and Rome*. Austin: University of Texas Press, 2013.

Portella, Ivana Della. *The Appian Way: From Its Foundation to the Middle Ages*. Los Angeles: The J. Paul Getty Museum, 2004.

Ramage, Nancy H. and Andrew Ramage. *Roman Art*. New York: Prentice-Hall, 2008.

Rives, James B. *Religion in the Roman Empire*. London: Wiley-Blackwell, 2006.

Shelton, Jo-Ann, ed. and trans. *As The Romans Did: A Sourcebook in Roman Social History*. New York: Oxford University Press, 1998.

Solomon, Jon. *The Ancient World in the Cinema*. New York: A.S. Barnes and Company, 2001.

Southern, Pat. *The Roman Army: A Social and Institutional History*. New York: Oxford University Press, 2007.

Staccioli, Romolo Augusto. *The Roads of the Romans*. Los Angeles: The J. Paul Getty Museum, 2004.

Syme, Ronald. *The Roman Revolution*. New York: Oxford University Press, 2002.

Tuck, Steven L. *A History of Roman Art*. New York: Wiley Blackwell, 2015.

Turner, Tracey. *Hard Nuts of History: Ancient Rome*. London: A & C Black, 2014.

Ward, Allen M. and Fritz M. Heichelheim. *A History of the Roman People*. London: Pearson, 2013.

Watkins, Richard. *Gladiator*. Boston: Houghton Mifflin, 2000.

Zanker, Paul. *Roman Art*. Los Angeles: The J. Paul Getty Museum, 2010.

About the Author

Classical historian and award-winning author Don Nardo has written numerous acclaimed volumes about ancient civilizations and peoples. They include studies of the histories, cultures, and mythologies of the Sumerians, Babylonians, Egyptians, Minoans, Greeks, Romans, Persians, Celts, and others. Nardo, who also composes and arranges orchestral music, lives with his wife Christine in Massachusetts.

INDEX

Acta Diurna, 12
Alexander the Great, 52
animals, 30, 35–36, 40–48, 49
aqueducts, 21
arcades, 20–21
arches, 18–19, 20, 21
architecture, 17, 18, 26
Astley, Philip, 47–48
Augustus (emperor), 9, 11, 59

bathhouses, 14, 17
books, 12–13, 27
Bordeaux Itinerary, 27
braziers, 13
bridges, 18, 21–22

Caesar, Julius, 15
calendar, 15
cambering, 24
Carpophorus (hunter), 45
chariots, 17, 24, 30, 35–36
Christians, 27, 38, 42
circuses, 17, 18, 20–21, 30, 40, 41,
    47–48
codices, 13
Colosseum, 19, 20, 32, 33, 45
concrete, 16, 19–20

Domitian (emperor), 39

emperors, 9, 11, 33, 38, 39, 45, 59

firefighters, 9–10
Flamininus, Titus (general), 54
food, 10–11, 23, 25, 41

gladiators, 12, 17, 28–38, 39

heating, 13–14
hoplites, 52–53
housing, 7–8, 9, 13, 23
hunting, 41, 42–43, 44–45, 49
hypocausts, 13–14

insulae, 8, 9
itineraries, 27

Juvenal (poet), 8, 9

language, 58
ludi, 32

maniples, 53–54, 55
milestones, 25
military, 23, 50–58, 59
movies, 29, 38

newspapers, 12

Orata, Gaius Sergius, 13

phalanxes, 52–53, 54
Philip V (Greek king), 54
pila, 52
pompae, 33, 38
Pompeii, 11
popinae, 10
population, 7
posting stations, 25, 27

religion, 27, 38, 42, 58
roads, 16, 21, 22–24, 25–26, 27
ruins, 11, 19, 26, 32

Severus, Septimius (emperor), 39
slavery, 9–10, 13, 23, 30, 31, 43, 45
social welfare, 11
stadiums, 16–18, 19, 20, 26, 28, 32, 33,
    41, 45

thermopolii, 10
Titus (emperor), 45
training, 31, 32, 43, 45–47, 55
Trajan (emperor), 44

vaults, 19
venatores, 43, 44–45, 47, 49
Via Appia, 24

water, 10, 21
women, 39, 42, 43, 46